It's the Awkwardness for Me

12 Ways to Make Being a Teen Less Awkward

Maeve Ronan

DEDICATION

For the 16 year old who's wondering if she will ever be good enough.

CONTENTS

LET'S START HERE

Whether you've had embarrassing moments you'll never forget, panic every time you have a conversation, or adopted awkwardness as a personality trait, awkward is probably a word you know too well.

I'm right there with you. Awkward memories from my childhood still haunt me, especially from my middle and high school years. I've been through many of the things you're going through now, and I know how isolating it can feel.

Contrary to what you've been told, you don't have to suffer through your awkward teen years alone. There are tools and strategies you can use so awkwardness doesn't derail your entire life. I'm in my 20s now and can safely say that had I read a book like this sooner, my middle and high school experience would have been drastically different.

You'll learn how to stay calm in awkward moments, what to say in awkward conversations, and how to carry yourself more confidently around others, even if you feel insecure. If that sounds like something you need, then keep reading. You're about to learn how to be less awkward.

ONE MORE THING

Before we get to the good stuff, let's get on the same page. I'm not a perfect human. I'm not even a doctor or therapist; I'm just someone who has learned a thing or two since being a teenager. While I sincerely hope these strategies help you as they did for me, they might not be right for everyone. It's up to you to decide what next steps to take. After all, you are the author of your own life.

I was the shy, studious kid in school. I didn't feel connected with any of my classmates, so I rarely spoke up. I thought no one wanted to hear what I had to say, even though my mind was bursting with ideas.

I always thought people were looking at my poofy hair, my weird outfit, or my acne. I spent most of my time with headphones on, buried in a book, trying to make myself as invisible as possible.

My home life didn't help. My parents were going through a divorce, and both of my closest grandparents passed away suddenly. My mental health spiraled, and I went from asking to go to a friend's house to begging to see a therapist. It was scary because I didn't know what was going on with me— my thoughts were out of control. I felt like no one loved me and I struggled to see the point of living. I could no longer trust anyone, and it felt like the world was conspiring against me.

I isolated myself from any resemblance of friends I had and lost touch with my sisters too. It was a difficult time in my life that didn't need to get as dark as it did. I wish I had someone by my side, outside of the mess, who could have helped me get through it.

Looking back on it now, the worst part wasn't even what happened; it was the loneliness. I became so depressed and anxious because I didn't know how to cope with all of the dramatic life changes. While I can't go back and change what happened, I can share with you everything I wish I knew back then.

To give you hope if you're in those sucky middle and high school years right now, my life did get way better. I went from feeling alone, depressed, and chronically overwhelmed to feeling supported, excited, and ready to take on any challenge. After finally graduating high school, I went to college, where I met new friends and tried out new activities. I left school early to expand my horizons and explore the world. I lived in Ireland and traveled to places I never imagined, like Bali and Thailand. I learned so much about life from interviewing over 100 accomplished and successful individuals on what they wish they knew when they were younger. Ranging from entrepreneurs to artists to scientists to even billionaires, their colorful and unique insights changed my entire paradigm. You'll hear from a few of them throughout this book.

After building my own conversation skills and self-esteem, I started to notice that life was more awesome than I previously thought. The world was bigger than I realized and people were more complex than I assumed. I became excited to fully experience life, challenges and all, rather than hide from my problems.

A transformation like this can happen for you too. You won't always be where you are now. Life is long and you will grow as a person. You may even rekindle relationships with your family members if they aren't great right now. It is possible for your life to improve. You can get closer to who you want to be by taking small steps each day.

Let's take the first step together by learning how to deal with cringe-worthy awkward moments. Once we tackle awkwardness, you'll be well on your way to becoming the person you've always dreamed of being.

ACCEPT REALITY

It's the Awkwardness for Me

It's a Part of Life

You're always going to experience awkward moments in life. It doesn't matter how confident you become, how pretty you are, or even what college you get into. There will always be random weird situations you find yourself in. The only way to avoid awkwardness all together would be to hide away your entire life, which would not be fun... at all. In becoming independent (which is honestly so awesome and not as scary as it sounds), you will face rejection and embarrassment. That's just a part of life, and it means you're growing up.

If you try to avoid all awkward moments, you'll miss out on the most amazing parts of life— like discovering what interests you, traveling to fascinating places, and meeting new people. Instead, arm yourself with self-improvement techniques, so you are resilient enough to get through anything.

I'm not here to sell you a false hope that you can become so incredible you never have to be awkward again. It's the opposite. The more you push yourself to become better, the more you'll find yourself in new, and potentially awkward, situations. Don't worry though, the sense of accomplishment you gain and the new opportunities you find after trying something new make it all worth it.

Here's your first step to becoming less awkward: Accept that awkward moments happen, and that's okay.

By understanding awkwardness is a part of life, you won't be so alarmed when embarrassing moments happen. You'll be able to keep your cool if you're in a sticky situation and handle it with ease. Don't freak out; embrace it.

It's okay if you feel uncomfortable and insecure right now instead of confident. Everyone else feels like that too, especially in middle and high school. Over time you will rise above those feelings, and with some new strategies, you will become confident sooner than you think.

Even though awkwardness is a part of life for everyone, at your life stage, it is dramatically heightened. You are not going crazy when you feel super awkward compared to people in college or in their 20s. You probably *are* more awkward than them. Sorry, but it's the truth!

You feel like that because you're in a weird life stage where you don't know how to carry yourself, speak up for yourself, and appreciate yourself. It's the worst. You won't always feel that insecure.

When you become more sure of yourself, a lot of that awkwardness will naturally go away. While awkward moments are a part of life, they can become way less nerve-wracking.

You're Not Alone

You're not the only one who is awkward. I know it might *feel* like that, but everyone else feels like that too.

I've taught and mentored hundreds of students over the past five years, and it always surprises me how many teens share the same insecurities, yet struggle alone. I used to do that too. I thought I was the only one who felt so awkward, especially in school. It turns out, we have a lot more in common than we think.

While I was in Bali interviewing accomplished individuals, I met Victoria Bauman, a successful life and breath coach who travels all around the world. When I asked her what advice she would give her younger self, she said this:

"As a teenager, I was very self-conscious and had low self-esteem. You wouldn't necessarily know from the outside because I pretended that I had it all together. In high school, I would walk through the hallways with my head down because I was worried about what people thought about me.

"Having low self-esteem was so painful because I was constantly questioning myself. I had bad skin too, so that didn't help. I wish I could go back and tell my younger self that everybody is questioning themselves and that everybody is struggling on the inside. My perception as a teenager was that certain people had everything figured out and were cruising through life. I wanted to be like them and have it all figured out.

"I thought there was something wrong with me. What I didn't know was that they too were battling their own struggles and insecurities. If I could go back, I would want myself to understand that everyone else goes through that weird teenage phase too. That would've taken a lot of the pressure off."

Now, Victoria is such a driven and confident woman inspiring others to live their most authentic lives, but she was insecure as a teen. Those confident people you admire feel awkward too. The reason they seem so confident is because they don't let little awkward moments define them. They brush it off, move on, and aren't thinking about it for the rest of the day.

You are living in a season of self-discovery, which is bound to come with awkward moments. The people around you are living through it too. Instead of agonizing over embarrassing moments, try having meaningful conversations with others around you to see if they can relate. They'll probably be grateful you brought it up.

There are 7.7 billion people in the world, did you really think you could be the only awkward one? Think again, you are in great company.

AWKWARD OR AWESOME?

Being awkward can actually help you. Hear me out, isn't that half of what TikTok is? We love seeing behind the scenes when things go wrong. Mistakes happen to all of us, and honestly, they make you seem more relatable and approachable.

Sometimes what we consider awkward can even be our most unique qualities. It's not awkward that you look or speak differently than everyone else. It's not even a bad thing if you're silly sometimes or if you make a mistake. It adds to your charm. Embrace it. It's more fun to be around someone who is completely themselves and isn't concerned about what other people think.

If you're awkward occasionally, it helps other people let down their guard and trust you more. It even gives them the freedom to be their authentic selves around you too.

Chip Wilson, the founder of Lululemon, shared a similar thought when I asked him what he would tell his younger self. He said this:

"Everyone is a snowflake, and nature makes you that way to fulfill different niches of society. Whatever you are thinking is perfect. You don't have to, nor should you, have the same thoughts as anyone else. You don't have to do anything your parents, friends or society thinks you 'should' do, as this will hinder your individualism and inhibit your greatness."

Stop trying to be like everyone else and let your individuality shine through! The goal isn't to look like a perfect influencer; it's to look like you. Don't strive for fakeness, strive for authenticity. Take it from Mr. Wilson, he literally invented yoga pants. When all other athletic fashion looked the same, he dared to be different. Not only is it okay to stand out, but it also may lead you to great success.

Just because you're a little different than those around you, that doesn't mean you are out of place. Faiza Muhammad, a language expert and entrepreneur, helped me understand this when we met at a women's leadership conference in Bali. She was translating everything from Balinese to English and English to Balinese. It was so awesome, I knew I had to meet her after the event and hear her story.

When I asked Faiza what advice she would give her younger self, she said this:

"I would tell the younger version of myself that some of the things I focused on obsessively are just a part of being a teen. Most of them don't really matter.

"Be the truest version of yourself. You don't have to fit in because if you don't, there's probably a good reason for that. This is a colorful world full of different people, and you don't always have to fit in.

"You don't have to be good at everything. If you're bad at something, then maybe it's just not part of your gift, and you should focus on what you can do well. Be more productive and stop beating yourself up over something you're not great at."

Some of those things you're worrying about, like what someone else thought of that sentence you said in class, really don't matter! Move on. Free yourself.

It's okay not to be good at everything, and it's okay not to fit in. Appreciate your uniqueness rather than resist it. Maybe those awkward parts of you are actually the most awesome parts of you.

How to Make Being a Teen Less Awkward: ACCEPT REALITY

1. Understand that awkward moments are a part of life.

2. Know that you are never alone.

3. Appreciate the unique parts about yourself.

It's the Awkwardness for Me

LEARN STRATEGIES

When You Embarrass Yourself

If you're anything like I was as a teenager, one embarrassing moment can ruin your entire day. What happens when you get embarrassed— do you tear up and run to the bathroom? Maybe you burrow under your pillows and hide in bed for the rest of the day, endlessly scrolling on your phone.

Even though you might be able to get away with your current coping mechanisms, you won't be able to forever. What happens when you get a job and need to be at work for the rest of your shift? Or if you're on a weekend road trip with friends? In the real world, you can't just hide from your problems. You have to learn how to stay calm in the moment and persevere.

Let's learn some strategies that'll help you not let embarrassing moments ruin your day. Soon, you'll be able to brush them off like they are no big deal. I know it might seem highly impossible, like you're the only one this won't work on, but just try them out and see how they work for you.

#1
Laugh it off

If you did something kind of funny and everyone is laughing, just laugh with them, even if you are dying inside. Honestly, the less of a deal you make out of it, the sooner people will move on. This is usually a good method to use in a group of people you don't know well or friends who always find something new to talk about.

Don't take yourself too seriously. Whether it's tripping up the stairs or mispronouncing a word, everyone messes up sometimes. Even if you're secretly freaking out, don't let it show. If you respond with defensiveness, that will escalate the situation and turn it into something it doesn't have to be. Laughing helps convince your brain that everything is okay.

If you're in a situation where people keep bringing it up and poking fun at you, you'll need additional strategies to get them off your back, but we'll touch on that later. For now, use the laughing it off strategy for any minor awkward moment that people will forget about minutes later. The calmer and more lighthearted you can remain, the quicker your bystanders will move on.

#2
Call it out

Another option for how to react in an awkward situation is to call it out. This is perfect to use when other people saw what you just did, but no one says anything, so it's weird and quiet. Calling it out ends the silence and allows people to breathe and acknowledge what just happened.

Only use this strategy if you're the one who did something awkward. If the awkwardness is coming from someone else, let them decide if they want to draw attention to it or not. Otherwise, you might seem rude.

This technique puts you in control of the narrative. No one else can make fun of you because you already pointed out your mistake. By calling it out and laughing it off, you give everyone the green light to move on.

Here's an example:

If you mispronounced a word while reading aloud in class, you could just say, "Wow, I just said that, haha, I mean [correct pronunciation]."

The key part of this technique is after calling it out, move on! If you continue to point out your flaws, you will make yourself look worse. This isn't a strategy to use too often; you don't want to be overly self-depreciative. Use this one sparingly, only in those scenarios where other people are waiting for you to address what just happened.

You train others how to treat you. Instead of leaving the door open for someone else to tease you, call it out, then indicate the moment is over by moving on. No one will stop to point it out again because you already have.

#3
Pretend it never happened

Most people don't even notice your awkward moments! You might think they are glaringly obvious, and others care about everything you do. They don't. Trust me, I spent years agonizing about what others think of me, only to discover they don't think of me. Most of the time no one notices, and if they do, they really don't care.

If something very minor happens, don't even bring it up. Why bother bringing attention to it? Brush it off. Like if your voice cracks or something, just keep going. Things like that happen to everyone, so don't make it a bigger deal than it needs to be.

If you try to ignore it and people make fun of you, be unbothered. People taunt others to get a reaction. If their comment doesn't faze you, they'll get bored and stop. No one likes to laugh at someone who isn't embarrassed. Just ignore it and move on. Even better, as you develop confidence, you'll give off a signal to those around you not to poke fun at you.

The key part about pretending your awkward moments never happened is to not obsess over them. You can't carry them around in your head for the rest of the day. The whole point is to give yourself freedom to move on, not to continue carrying that burden!

Moving on is always the best option when someone else does something awkward. Out of respect for them, pretend it never happened. It doesn't help to bring attention to it, even if people laugh a little. Sometimes things don't need to be said, just leave it be.

I know you probably want to avoid awkward situations all together, but at least when they do happen, you'll have 3 options for how to respond and keep going with your day.

CHANNEL FUTURE YOU

When people try to help you through a stressful situation, they usually tell you not to worry. While the advice itself isn't bad, has anyone ever told you *how* to not worry?

One of the most helpful strategies to worry less when something embarrassing happens is to envision what your future self would do. Even though you might not know how to manage your anxious thoughts right now, your future self does. Think about the ideal person you want to become someday. They are so much more confident, experienced, and sure of themselves. When you channel that version of you, their energy and skills can help you get through any awkward situation.

When you are in an awkward moment, ask yourself:

What would future me do?

When you pretend you are your future self, it tricks your brain. You are no longer an awkward scrawny middle schooler but a confident and kind 20-year-old. When something awkward happens, don't bow your head in fear; be the bold version of yourself.

Not sure what future you looks like yet? Take some time to brainstorm. The first book in this series, *It's the Depression for Me,* has some exercises to help you envision who you want to become.

It might feel weird at first to act so differently than your usual self, especially when you have little self-esteem, but soon it won't be out of character. Eventually, you will grow into that better, future version of yourself.

LOOK FORWARD

While tools for what to do in the moment are super helpful, sometimes the most unbearable part of an awkward moment is when you are left alone, replaying the events of the day over and over again. The worst thing you can do is turn one awkward moment into an entire week of agony. If it was so dreadful, don't relive it repeatedly; release yourself from it!

Your thoughts dictate how you feel. To feel better, alter what thoughts you allow to live in your brain. When you are in an awkward moment, train yourself to immediately think, "This moment will pass." If your instinct is to feel like it's the end of the world, the moment will get worse. If you tell yourself this moment will pass, you will be able to stay calm.

Instead of thinking: "Omg, what did I just do? I can't believe I did that, I'm so awkward."

Try thinking: "This moment will pass. I am okay. It will be fine."

Whatever your mind hears in that moment will dictate how you act next. Feed your mind good thoughts, and good actions will follow. Find a positive anchor thought to hold onto, like "I am okay" or "This moment will pass."

Besides having an anchor thought, thinking about something you are excited for helps too. Even if you're looking forward to just being home at the end of the day, use that to your advantage.

Once the moment is over, it's okay to process what happened, but don't replay it endlessly. If nothing can be done to change it, set a timer. Give yourself time to sulk, to feel upset, and to replay the event. Write everything down in a journal.

When that timer goes off, let go of that moment. Times will vary based on severity, but it should be no longer than 30 minutes if it is something minor.

You might be thinking to yourself, how can I let go? This is where practice comes in. You can't just read this book and expect a miracle cure. You have to practice letting go. When those menacing thoughts come back into your mind, you have to tell them to stop and to go away. You must decide you would rather experience the freedom from letting go rather than the distress from being upset. This can be hard to get the hang of, but you'll get better at it with practice.

Honestly, I could never fully accomplish letting go of my anxious thoughts until I believed in God. Knowing there is a holy being in control took a lot of the pressure off me to be perfect. I'm not about to preach the gospel to you, but there is something to be said about the calmness that comes from having someone to give your burdens to.

No matter what you believe, as you keep practicing you will get better at moving on. You will feel unfazed by moments that used to destroy you. You've got this. Keep looking forward. This too shall pass.

It's the Awkwardness for Me

DON'T BE A FOOL

Sometimes there will be people who intentionally want to make you look awkward. Whether it's to embarrass you or belittle you, it's not always fair. You can't control how other people act, but you can control how you act.

The best way to combat someone making fun of you is to have an insane amount of confidence. You have to know how to stand up for yourself. This doesn't mean having a loud mouth in front of people, it's about having a sureness of yourself, so other people's blows don't knock you down.

If someone intentionally says something to make you look bad, always take the high road. If you lash out, you're the one who just made yourself look like a fool. Don't do that.

Do this instead: Repeat what they said back to them in a curious tone, like you're asking an honest question. Doing that in a slow, confident manner is sometimes all it takes to make the other person accountable for what they just said to you.

Here's an example:

If someone says to you, in a snarky tone, "Did you seriously just say that?" you would pause and then say, "Did I seriously just say that?" in a totally non-snarky tone.

Just pause as if that is such a peculiar question to ask somebody. If they say nothing, respond, "I guess I did, [Name], thanks for asking."

They will feel like the odd one for even mentioning it. Remember, this is not meant to be said spitefully or sarcastically. Just say it as bland as you can, without a care in the world, like "Huh, I don't even know what you're saying."

Here's another example:

If someone makes an unnecessary comment, such as, "Having a bad hair day?"

After pausing to think about what they just asked, respond in a confused tone, "Having a bad hair day?"

Then wait, so they are the ones expected to respond and explain themselves. Just seem stunned and astounded that someone would even ask that.

If they respond with something rude, you have two options. You can choose not to answer, or you can ask another question. The second option is bolder and it'll indicate how they're acting is not okay, and you will not tolerate it. In that scenario, here are a few options of what you could say:

"Do you think that's an appropriate question to ask me?"

"What kind of question is that?" insulte

"How would you like it if someone asked you that?"

The key here is not to blame or get angry. Just state it like it's a simple question that doesn't even deserve your full energy. Let them figure it out; they're the ones who put themselves in that situation. And then move on— their negativity is not your problem. Being unbothered is the best comeback

How to Make Being a Teen Less Awkward: Learn Strategies

4. Channel future you in embarrassing situations.

5. Know the moment will end; set a timer and look forward.

6. Realize your thoughts affect how you feel; let the unhelpful ones go. "im ok, ill be fine"

7. Be unbothered when others try to make you look awkward.

It's the Awkwardness for Me

BE PREPARED

It's the Awkwardness for Me

HAVE A PLAN

If you know awkward moments will happen, you might as well be prepared for them. I used to get super anxious when something awkward happened and angry when something annoying happened. Sometimes I still do, but I have a plan to make sure it doesn't escalate.

When I feel frustrated or anxious because of something, I tell myself, "I know this isn't fair and it's really annoying, but God is so good, and there are way better things to be focused on. This is one little moment that will pass. I can let it go. Me getting upset or calling them out isn't going to help. Letting it go is the better option."

If I'm alone, I might allow myself one little scream or to shed one tear, and then I look forward to something I'm excited about and decide I'm moving on. That's my plan for when anything catches me off guard. Your plan might look different.

Your plan might even differ depending on what situation you're in. Some conversations are bound to be awkward before they even begin, so your plan needs to account for that. This could happen with parents, teachers, or employers.

Remember that just because a conversation might be awkward, that is not a reason to avoid it; it is probably a sign to have it sooner! Get it over with so you aren't carrying that stress. The sooner you make it happen, the sooner it will be over.

If your teacher incorrectly marks something on your test, and you have to bring it up to them, do it within the day you get the test. If you wait too long, you'll overthink it and never do it. If you struggle with overthinking and procrastinating, you might like a strategy from speaker Mel Robbins. It's called the 5 second rule, where you countdown 5, 4, 3, 2, 1 and then blast off and go take action. Essentially, you're doing what you need to before your mind takes over by thinking too much. There's a video of Mel Robbins explaining it on MaeveRonan.com if you want to learn more.

If it's an important conversation, like negotiating a pay raise or asking your parents for more independence, do some prep before. Know what you will say and practice saying it. Be clear on what you believe, what the other person might think, and what you want the outcome to be. This helps you better communicate your message. It's much better to be clear than avoid what you're trying to say because you're too nervous.

Think about awkward scenarios you typically find yourself in, especially those that upset you the most, and come up with a plan that will help calm you and resolve it quickly.

Ask Better Questions

Have you ever tried to have a conversation, and it just falls flat? It's easy to blame the other person, but maybe you're asking the wrong questions. It's up to you to prepare for future conversations by learning how to ask better questions.

When you know how to ask good questions, you won't be stressed about what to say next. Often we think conversations are about knowing what to share about ourselves. In reality, it's more about knowing what to *ask* of someone else.

People love talking about themselves. If you know how to get other people talking about themselves, you'll even be more well-liked. Have a few go-to questions you can use in any situation. These are three of my favorites:

"What made you want to do that?"

"Did you always know you wanted to do that?"

"Is that something you've always done?"

The first question is great for when someone shares about making a big decision, like going into a new career or course. Instead of asking questions about *what* they're doing, inquire about *why* they're doing it, and you'll get more interesting responses.

The second and third questions are perfect when asking someone about passions, career, or hobbies. They'll usually give you a one word answer when you ask *what* they do, and then you can swoop in and be curious *how* they became involved in that. They'll tell you a story of how they got into that line of work or developed those passions. Ask your teachers if they always knew they wanted to teach, and see what they say. You might be surprised by their answers.

Don't forget that after you ask the first question, you have to keep asking more! You can share a little about yourself when the moment comes up, but then keep going. Remember that the person you're talking to probably hasn't read this book, so they might not know how to keep a conversation going either.

Take the lead and allow them to talk. Honestly, it doesn't matter what the topic is, and you can change it from one question to the next. If you stay curious to learn more about the hidden stories of others, you will always have something to say.

'

BELIEVE IN YOURSELF

The absolute best way to prepare is to build up your self-belief and confidence so much that no embarrassing moment will catch you off guard. I know it sounds cliché to believe in yourself, and it's probably something you've heard before, but hear me out.

Envision what it would feel like if you wholeheartedly believed in yourself. What if you didn't criticize and doubt yourself every minute? What if you cheered yourself on through every struggle? What if those self-deprecating thoughts didn't take over when something goes wrong?

Often we are our worst critics and cause more stress for ourselves than necessary. When we let our negative and panicky thoughts dictate how we feel, chaos and depression ensue. When we learn to look at a situation objectively, with reason rather than with our emotions, we realize that everything will be okay.

When you believe in yourself, you don't care as much about what others think. Little awkward moments won't bother you anymore because you have better things to think about.

Someone who embodies this self-belief is Khanita Khoon, an awesome woman I met from Northern Thailand. Pharmacist and entrepreneur, Khanita now owns her own pharmacy. She recognized from a young age that she had to advocate for herself if she wanted to become someone in this world. When there was no one in her rural town to see her talent, she worked hard to make it to the big city, and eventually other countries around the world. During our interview, I asked her what teens should do if they feel like no one believes in them, and she said this:

"Nobody is going to find you. If you are waiting for somebody to find you, it will take ages, especially if you are hidden in the mountains of Thailand like me. You have to present yourself and find your own way up.

"One thing you can do is know what you're capable of. Know your specialty. I know I am an expert in biomedical engineering, so I found a community related to that. You have to find a society or business, preferably the biggest or most respected one, and find a way to get in. That's what I did with IEEE Engineering in Medicine and Biology Society, the largest medical society in the world.

"You can start small and slow. Participate first as a student. Observe the speakers, learn where they came from and how they got there. Figure out who's in charge of the conference and get to know the staff. I helped sell T-shirts at first. The staff started recognizing me after I sold 100 T-shirts.

"A year later, I helped with student activities. I started spending time around CEOs of tech startups and biomedical engineering companies. There are opportunities where you can have lunch with these people. You have to join and be a part of the conversation. Be friendly, say 'Hi' to everyone.

"Most people are very tense at these conferences. I would try to get them to loosen up and open up a bit. One time, I walked around with a bunny ear headband with blinking lights just to make people smile. Most people sit with their friends, so I always invited others to come sit at my table.

"There's a lot of diversity at conferences like this, as people come from all over the world. Everybody has their own strengths. Never undermine who you are and where you come from, especially when talking to people from more famous universities or more senior positions."

Even when Khanita was a complete beginner, she believed that someday she could become an expert. She started by asking questions, listening, and getting involved. All three things you can do too! Don't let being young stop you— people love to help the next generation of leaders.

Plus, you have the internet on your side. Your phone is way more than just a time-waster; it's literally your ticket to learn anything and connect with anyone. Even if you don't know exactly the career you want, you can still learn about different opportunities.

You have the tools. Now, it's up to you to do the research to find those opportunities where you can learn and grow. You won't learn from the sidelines. Once you're participating, you can meet more people who will help you on your journey.

It's the Awkwardness for Me

Surround Yourself with Winners

It can be hard to believe in yourself when the people around you constantly bring each other down. It can be even harder when you've never seen someone genuinely believe in themselves to model yourself after.

Just because you currently have no good role models, that does not mean you can't find people to look up to. Think about teachers and coaches in your life, maybe a dance teacher or school counselor. Spend more time with them rather than people who bring you down.

If you can't find anyone, use your phone to find people living the life you want to live. They can be your role models too; just choose wisely. Jim Rohn, one of the most successful self-improvement speakers, said you become the average of the five people you spend the most time with. It's up to you to choose who your five people are.

Like Khanita shared, no one is coming to find you. It's not your fault where you were born, but it is your responsibility to seek people you want to resemble. Find others in groups that succeed and learn from them, not the people in your hometown who complain about how awful life is.

There are others living the life you want to live, and sometimes all it takes for us to believe is to learn about them. This happened for John Hope Bryant, American author and entrepreneur. He shared with me that one of the most pivotal moments in his life was when a businessman came into his classroom during career day at school. I asked him what was going through his head in that moment, and he said this:

"It's one of the most important questions you could ask because nothing physically changed. My environment didn't change. The classroom didn't change. The fact that he was white and I was black hadn't changed. My bank account hadn't gotten any bigger. I mean, none of that changed. But everything else changed. The endorphins firing on the right side of my brain changed. My level of hope and optimism changed. My belief in myself changed. My confidence changed. My inspiration and aspiration absolutely changed.

"When this banker came into my classroom, I asked him, 'What do you do for a living? And how did you get rich legally?'

"I had never seen a guy like this before… he had a blue suit, a white shirt, and a red tie. He was Caucasian, and he wasn't a detective. He had a nice car, and it wasn't stolen. He made a lot of money, and it was legal. He paid his taxes and had a business card. His business was transparent, and everybody could understand he was on a salary.

"This was all stunning to me. He even worked in a skyscraper. There are no skyscrapers in Compton, California, except a multistory building called the courthouse.

"So I said to him, 'Sir, I don't get it.'

"He said, 'Young man, this is easy. I'm a banker, and I finance entrepreneurs.'

"I said, 'I don't know what an entrepreneur is, but if you're financing them and it's legal, I'm going to be one.' And that interaction just scripted my entire life."

All Mr. Bryant needed to believe in himself was to see what was possible for him. That one interaction inspired him to start multiple businesses, write several books, and start a non-profit that equips people with financial tools and education to become financially independent.

Today could be that day for you. You've read about people in this book living cool lives. Look them up, do more research, and reach out to them. No matter how crazy your dream sounds, there's someone out there living it right now. Seek those people who have done it before you and learn from them. Whatever you are dreaming of is possible!

Trick Your Mind

Throughout this book, we have covered a lot of practical tips and strategies to be less awkward. In this final chapter, you'll find a bunch of little tips. They are physical things you can do to trick your body into thinking you are calm and confident. They sound simple, but they are incredibly effective, especially the more you do them.

If you are serious about improving your life, keep yourself accountable by using a journal to track every time you catch yourself in a bad habit.

Keep your shoulders back!
It gives off an air of confidence.

Keep your chin up!
Don't bow your head; you are not ashamed of who you are and who you are becoming. Keep your head up even if you don't feel like it.

Stop fidgeting!
Checking your hair and clothes indicates to others that you are nervous. Don't let them see you sweat.

Stop looking around to see what people think of you!
They're not thinking of you. :)

Sit up straight!
Good posture is essential.

Keep your hair out of your face!
Don't hide yourself. You are beautiful, even if you don't recognize it yet.

Smile!
When you smile, it does two things:
1. Convinces your brain you're happy
2. Convinces others you're enjoyable to be around

Smile even with those braces. And don't worry about wrinkles; you want your face to show how well you lived when you get older, not to be a boring blank canvas.

Act as if!

Acting as if is something we talked about in the first book in this series, *It's the Depression for Me*. Act as if you were confident, and over time, you will be.

Just like anything, you must practice these before they become second nature. Start by using a journal and write down your goals for the day and week. Write down every time you catch yourself frowning, bowing your head, or fidgeting. Write down every time you correct yourself so you can replace it with a healthier habit. You will improve before you know it.

How to Make Being a Teen Less Awkward: Be Prepared

8. Have a plan for awkward situations.

9. Improve your conversations by asking better questions.

10. Recognize that believing in yourself matters.

11. Look up to people you want to become like.

12. Replace your negative habits with better ones.

You Did It

You finished the book! Maybe that's no big deal for you, or maybe this is the first book you've finished since 4th grade. Either way, I'm proud of you. If this book helped you, would you share it with someone who could use it, like a friend or even a family member? You never know, it could change their life. Leave your review on Amazon to help inspire other teens too!

Now that you have these insights, what should you do? I hate to break it to you, but you can't just read a book and expect everything to magically get better. It's your turn to do the work. It's up to you to apply these concepts to your life.

I know it can feel overwhelming, even with a short book like this, but go back and pick just one section and focus on that for the next week. Don't try to change your entire life in one day. Pick one section and make a goal for yourself to make it happen. If you want accountability and to meet others with the same goals as you, head to MaeveRonan.com to join our community.

There's even a free 7-day plan you can download to kickstart your first week of becoming less awkward. You aren't alone. There are thousands of other teens right there with you.

If you're looking for more books, lucky for you, there's another one called *It's the Depression for Me*. It's all about how to stress less about your future and how to get excited about life again.

More books are coming soon. Until then, remember you can do this. You are exactly where you're meant to be, awkwardness and all. Take small steps each day to improve yourself. Life will get better if you genuinely put in the effort. You can become the person you've always dreamed of being. Even if you are super awkward right now, there is hope for you to become more graceful and confident. You've got this. Keep going.

ACKNOWLEDGEMENTS

Special thanks to my dad for being my most reliable and influential mentor. Thank you to my sister Molly and my mom for being my best, most loving supporters. Thank you to my interns for giving me feedback, and Heidi Kling for being a beta reader. Thanks to @MrProofreading for providing edits. Most importantly, thank you to my dear friend Morgan Frey for being by my side throughout this journey.

ABOUT THE AUTHOR

Maeve Ronan is the author of multiple relatable self-improvement books for teens. She believes that every teen should have the resources to succeed, regardless of their circumstances. Her books are based on what she wishes she knew in middle and high school, as well as insights from accomplished people around the world. Author of *It's the Depression for Me* and *It's the Awkwardness for Me*, Maeve Ronan plans to release her third book, *It's the Confidence for Me,* in November 2021.

To learn more about Maeve Ronan's story go to MaeveRonan.com.

SPECIAL THANKS TO MY BETA READERS

bellaring

.siann._

@Abigailbrandner

@alohavibesz

a.j

Abby

Abrandjoy10

adi marinov,12

Alexandra

Alexis Marie

Amalia

Amanda

Ana

Andrea K. Brinkman

Angie

Ari

Ash

Ashleigh

Audrey <3

Augustina

Ava .O

Ava the avocado

Beatriz

bethanyy :)

Blizzard

bre alldrin

Brianna/briicheesee

Brizaida G.C

Brydee

Camila

Camila Estrada :)

Carly Novack

Catharine Caldwell

Charlotte982

Chloe ♡

Chloe Levy

Claire

Cora Shinn

Daniella

Darbycakes1

Edith.m

eemilynicole.xo

eleana

Elena Radovic

Elina

ElinViolen

Ellen neff

Emilija

Emilija :)

Emily Sabine Wulf

Emina

emma

Erin

Eryn Blakely

Estere

Evely Evart

Faith

Frederikke

Frida _fridagirl_

Gabby Dorner

Gemma

Gisella Davis

Griffy

Gus Goodson

Gwyneth

Hannah @idkkhannah

Hayley____1

Hedda

Heidi K :)

Hope Elizabeth

Hope rose

Ingvill Mathilde

Inje_marie_

Isabella ferez <3

Jade B

Jagoda

Jamie

Jamilahz786

Janneke

jasmijn

Jayla<3

jaylen stephens

Jillianne.Irene

Joanne

joie

Joseph

Julia Zgherea

Kailany

Kaylie2006

Kendra Huggard

Kiah

Kiandra

Kiara

lana_lana2008

Larissa :)

Lauren MaKenzie :)

Leelia

Leelka

Leila

Leslie <3

Lidi @lidijathehuman

Lila<3

Liv

lotta

Maarit:)

Mac Burke

Madeleine

Madison McQ

Madison R. :)

Maisie<3

Matilda parker

Mia Erasmus

Micah_6424

mickey claire

Minne vc

Morgan <3

Mulan Anderson

Naazneen

Nea Willström

Netta Nissinen

Nika J:)

Nikola

Nina (Nikolina)

Nina

Norahvady

Nyree

Omeradoni

Oscar Ramirez

paytonmarie<3

petra

Potito

Reuben

Riot Hugo

Rowan

Rugilé

Salih/Salihkayan

Sanne van Os

Sara

Sarah

Sarahhhhhh

Sasha Donavan

Shae Meyer

shia/shia.caryy

Shyla

Sydney

Sydney_1902

Talia R

Theaaarsvoll

Tina Karolina Kalnipa

Valevale

Vanessa C.

Vera fall

Zainah Ott

Manufactured by Amazon.ca
Bolton, ON